The Healthy

Instant Pot Recipes

Healthy Recipes for Delicious and
Gorgeous Instant Pot Meals, Great
Vegetables and Meat Dishes for Live a
Life full of Energy

Victoria Carter

Table of Contents

broadly considered a truthful and accurate account of facts and as such, any inattention, use, or misuse of the information in question by the reader will render any resulting actions solely under their purview. There are no scenarios in which the publisher or the original author of this work can be in any fashion deemed liable for any hardship or damages that may befall them after undertaking information described herein. Additionally, the information in the following pages is intended only for informational purposes and should thus be thought of as universal. As befitting its nature, it is presented without assurance regarding its prolonged validity or interim quality. Trademarks that are mentioned are done without written consent and can in no way be considered an endorsement from the trademark holder.

Introduction

Instant pot is a pressure cooker, also stir-fry, stew, and cook rice, cook vegetables and chicken. It's an all-in-one device, so you can season chicken and cook it in the same pan, for example. In most cases, instant pot meals can be served in less than an hour.

Cooking less time is due to the pressure cooking function that captures the steam generated by the liquid cooking environment (including liquids released from meat and vegetables), boosts the pressure and pushes the steam back.

But don't confuse with traditional pressure cookers. The instant pot, unlike the pressure cooker used by grandparents, eliminates the risk of safety with a lid that locks and remains locked until pressure is released.

Even when cooking time is over in the instant pot, you need to take an additional step-to release the pressure.

There are two ways to relieve pressure. Due to the natural pressure release, the lid valve remains in the sealing position and the pressure will naturally dissipate over time. This process takes 20 minutes to over an hour, depending on what is cooked. Low fluidity foods (such as chicken wings) take less time than high fluidity foods such as soups and marinades.

Another option is manual pressure release (also called quick release). Now you need to carefully move the valve to the ventilation position and see that the steam rises slowly and the pressure is released. This Directions is much faster, but foods with high liquid content, such as soups, take about 15 minutes to manually relieve pressure.

Which option should I use? Take into account that even if natural pressure is released, the instant pot is still under pressure. This means that the food will continue to cook while the instant pot is in sealed mode. Manual pressure relief is useful when the dishes are well cooked and need to be stopped as soon as possible.

If the goal is to prepare meals quickly, set the cooking time for dishes that are being cooked in an instant pop and release the pressure manually after the time has passed.

Instant pots (called "Instapot" by many) are one of our favorite cookware because they can handle such a wide range of foods almost easily. Instant pots range from those that work on the basics of pressure cooking to those that can be sterilized using Suicide video or some models can be controlled via Wi-Fi.

In addition, if you want to expand the range of kitchenware, the Instant Pot brand has released an air fryer that can be used to make rotisserie chicken and homemade beef jerky. There is also an independent accumulator device that can be used in instant pots to make fish, steaks and more.

The current icon instant pot works like a pressure cooker and uses heat and steam to quickly cook food. Everything from perfect carnitas to boiled eggs was cooked, but not all ingredients and DIRECTIONSs work. Here are few foods that should not be cooked in classic instant pots.

Instant pots are not pressure fryer and are not designed to handle the high temperatures required to heat cooking oils like crispy fried chicken. Of course, the instant pot is great for dishes like Carnitas, but after removing the meat from the instant pot, to get the final crispness in the meat, transfer it to a frying pan for a few minutes or to an oven top and hot Crispy in the oven.

As with slow cookers, dairy products such as cheese, milk, and sour cream will pack into instant pots using pressure cooking settings or slow cooking settings. Do not add these ingredients after the dish are cooked or create a recipe in Instapot.

There are two exceptions. One is when making yogurt. This is merely possible if you are using an instant pot recipe. The other is only when making cheesecake and following an instant pot recipe.

Although you can technically cook pasta in an instant pot, gummy may appear and cooking may be uneven. To be honest, unless you have a choice, cooking pasta in a stove pot is just as fast and easy and consistently gives you better cooked pasta.

Instead of baking the cake in an instant pot, steam it. The cake is moist-it works for things like bread pudding-but there is no good skin on the cake or on the crunchy edge everyone fights with a baked brownie. However, let's say your desire is to build a close-up or a simple dessert with your family; you can get a damp sponge in about 30 minutes, except during the DIRECTIONS time.

Canning, a technique for cooking and sealing food in a jar, is often done in a pressure cooker. Therefore, it is recommended to create a batch of jam, pickles or jelly in Instapot. Please do not.

With an instant pot, you can't monitor the temperature of what you can, like a normal pressure cooker. In canning, it is important to cook and seal the dishes correctly. Incorrect cooking and sealing can lead to the growth of bacteria that can cause food poisoning.

If you want to avoid canning in an instant pot, some newer models, such as Duo Plus, have a sterilization setting that can clean kitchen items such as baby bottles, bottles and cookware.

Instant Pot Pressure Cooker Safety Tips

Instant Pot is a very safe pressure cooker consisting of various safety mechanisms. do not worry. It will not explode immediately. Most accidents are caused by user errors and can be easily avoided. To further minimize the possibility of an accident, we have compiled a list of safety tips.

1 Don't leave it alone

It is not recommended to leave home while cooking an instant pot. If you have to leave it alone, make sure it is under pressure and no steam is coming out.

2 Do not use KFC in instant pot

Do not fry in an instant pot or other pressure cooker.

KFC uses a commercial pressure fryer specially made to fry chicken (the latest one that operates at 5 PSI). Instant pots (10.5-11.6 PSI) are specially made to make our lives easier.

3 water intake!

Instant pots require a minimum of 1 1/2 cup liquid (Instant Pot Official Number) 1 cup liquid to reach and maintain pressure.

The liquid can be a combination of gravy, vinegar, water, chicken etc.

4 half full or half empty

The max line printed on the inner pot of the instant pot is not for pressure cooking.

For pressure cooking: up to 2/3 full

Food for pressure cooking that expands during cooking (grains, beans, dried vegetables, etc.): up to 1/2

5 Not a facial steamer

Deep cleaning is not performed even if the pressure cooker steam is used once.

When opening, always tilt the lid away from you. Wear waterproof and heat-resistant silicone gloves especially when performing quick release.

6 never use power

In situations of zero, you should try to force open the lid of the instant pot pressure cooker, unless you want to prevent a light saber from hitting your face.

7 Wash Up & Checkout

If you want to be secured, wash the lid after each use and clean the anti-block shield and inner pot. Make sure that the gasket (silicon seal ring) is in good shape and that there is no food residue in the anti-block shield before use.

Usually silicone seal rings should be replaced every 18-24 months. It is always advisable to keep extra things.

Do not purchase a sealing ring from a third party because it is an integral part of the safety features of the instant ring.

Using sealing rings that have not been tested with instant pot products can create serious safety concerns."

Before use, make sure that the sealing ring is securely fixed to the sealing ring rack and the anti-block shield is properly attached to the vapor discharge pipe.

A properly fitted sealing ring can be moved clockwise or counterclockwise in the sealing ring rack with little force.

With instant pots, the whole family can cook meals in less than 30 minutes. Cooked dishes such as rice, chicken, beef stew, sauce, yakitori can be cooked for 30-60 minutes from the beginning to the end. And yes, you can bake bread in an instant pot.

Old and ketogenic diet fans love instant pots for their ability to `` roast '' meat in such a short time, but vegetarians and vegans that can quickly cook dishes such as pumpkin soup, baked potatoes and marinated potato chilis, also highly appreciated oatmeal cream and macaroni and cheese.

Even dried beans, which usually require overnight cooking, can be prepared in 30 minutes to make spicy hummus.

Butternut Squash Soup

Preparation Time: 5 minutes

Cooking Time: 10 minutes

Servings: 4

Ingredients:

1 Peeled and diced Butternut squash.

1 Peeled and diced apple

1 Tbsp of Ginger powder or you can use pureed ginger

4 Cups of chicken broth

2 Tbsp of Coconut oil to taste

Directions:

Start by hitting the sauté button on the Instant you are using so that you pre-heat it.

When you become able to see the word "HOT", add the coconuts oil and add some of the butternut squash cubes to it then brown it ever lightly for approximately 5 minutes. Now, add the remaining quantity of squash and also add the rest of your ingredients.

Close; then lock your Instant Pot.

Now, press your manual and use the + for you to add 10 more minutes at high pressure to the cooking time.

When the time is over, open the instant pot by using the Quick Release.

Puree your mixture by using a blender right in your instant pot or you can also take the mixture out of the instant pot and place it into a blender. Serve and enjoy your delicious and healthy soup.

Nutrition:

Calories – 110

Protein – 2 g.

Fat – 2.5 g.

Carbs – 22 g.

Chicken Curry Soup

Preparation Time: 7 minutes

Cooking Time: 25 minutes

Servings: 3-4

Ingredients:

1 and ½ bone-in chicken halved breast

3 Diagonally sliced medium carrots

2 bay leaves

1 Pinch of Kosher salt

6 cups of low-sodium chicken broth

2 tablespoons of unsalted butter

1 thinly sliced large onion

1 teaspoon of sugar

1 and ½ teaspoons of Madras curry powder

1/3 Cup of jasmine rice

3 tablespoons of finely chopped fresh mint

3 tablespoons of chopped fresh dill

1 lemon sliced into thin wedges

Directions:

Combine your chicken, the carrots, the bay leaf and 1 pinch of salt into your Instant Pot.

Add around 3 cups of broth and press boil at a medium heat.

Close the lid and set at high pressure to around 10 to 15 minutes.

In the meantime; heat the quantity of butter over a medium low heat in a deep sauce pan.

Add the sugar and the onion with 1 pinch of salt and cook for around 5 minutes

Add the powder of curry and cook for around 2 minutes

When the timer beeps, add the broth and the rice; then set the heat to high and let simmer for 10 minutes

Remove the chicken out of the broth and shred the chicken meat into small pieces; then place it back in the broth.

Puree the mixture of the rice with a blender until it becomes smooth and then pour it into the mixture of the shredded chicken and the broth and let simmer for around 5 minutes

Once the soup is ready, garnish with herbs and then serve it with lemon

Enjoy!

Nutrition:

Calories – 147.2

Protein – 16 g. Fat – 5.1 g. Carbs – 7.6 g.

Asparagus Soup

Preparation Time: 6 minutes

Cooking Time: 10 minutes

Servings: 4

Ingredients:

½ lb of fresh asparagus cut into pieces. Make sure to remove the woody ends of the asparagus.

1 Sliced or chopped medium sized yellow onion.

3 Chopped or minced cloves of garlic cloves.

3 tbsp of coconuts oil.

½ teaspoon of dried thyme

5 Cups of bone broth

Zest + 1 Tbsp of juice of organic lemon

1 Teaspoon of sea salt

2 Cups of organic sour cream*

Directions:

Prepare your asparagus, the onion and the garlic.

Remove all the woody ends from the asparagus stalks and discard it.

Chop the asparagus into pieces of 1 inch each.

Slice the onion into halves and chop it.

Smash the garlic cloves or chop it.

Set the ingredients aside.

Place your stainless steel bowl inside your Instant Pot without putting the lid on it.

Put the instant potto the button "Sauté" and then add the coconut oil; the add onions and the garlic.

Cook the mixture for 5 minutes and keep stirring occasionally; add the thyme and the cook for 1 more minutes.

Add the broth, the asparagus and the lemon zest with the salt.

Lock the lid of the Instant pot and press the button "Manual" high pressure.

Set the pressure timer to 5 minutes and when the timer goes off, add the sour cream and stir; of course after the instant pot releases the steam.

Serve and enjoy

Nutrition:

Calories – 161.2

Protein – 6.3 g.

Fat – 8.2 g.

Carbs – 16.4 g.

Lentil Soup

Preparation Time: 6 minutes

Cooking Time: 10 minutes

Servings: 4

Ingredients:

1 Big diced onion

3minced garlic cloves

2 Tbsp of red curry paste

1/8 Teaspoon of ginger powder

1 Tbsp of red pepper flakes

1 and ½ oz Can coconut milk

1 oz Can of cut tomatoes

2 Cups of broth (Vegetable broth)

1 and ½ Cups of Red lentils

Spinach

Directions:

In your Instant Pot cooker, click the button of the option "Sauté" and wait a couple of minutes until it becomes warm.

Now, add your diced onion and the garlic; then sauté altogether until the components become brown. Add a little quantity of broth.

Once you notice the ingredients starting to have a brown colour, press the cancelling button to stop the process of sautéing.

Add the paste of the red curry, the ginger powder and the red pepper flakes and keep stirring.

Add your coconut milk, the diced tomatoes, the vegetable broth and the lentils and stir again.

Now, lock the lid and the button "Manual" then reduce your timer to around 7 minutes.

Let the pressure in the pot release naturally.

Once the steam is released, open the Instant Pot and add the spinach

Serve and enjoy your soup.

Nutrition:

Calories – 120

Protein – 8 g.

Fat – 1.5 g.

Carbs – 20 g.

Potato Soup

Preparation Time: 5 minutes

Cooking Time: 30 minutes

Servings: 5

Ingredients:

6 medium peeled and diced potatoes

¾ Cup of sliced baby carrots

½ Can of Progresso Creamy Garlic

½ Cup of chopped celery

½ Cup of fresh and chopped baby spinach leaves

1 Cup of chopped onion

1 Cup of broth

1/8 Teaspoon of crushed red pepper

1/8 Teaspoon of paprika

1 Tbsp of ground flax or you can use chia seeds

½ Teaspoon of salt

Sharp grated cheddar cheese

Basil leaves

Directions:

Place all of your ingredients inside your Instant Pot and mix them very well.

Lock the led and set the button to Soup and set your timer to 30 minutes.

Once done, place a towel on the lid and try a fast pressure release; then insert your blender to immerse and keep repeating the same procedure until your soup become thick.

Taste your soup and add a pinch of salt if needed. Serve your soup and enjoy it with Serve whole grain wheat bread.

Nutrition:

Calories – 208

Protein – 8.3 g.

Fat – 6.1 g.

Carbs – 28 g.

Cauliflower Soup

Preparation Time: 5 minutes

Cooking Time: 30 minutes

Servings: 5

Ingredients:

4 Cups of vegetable broth (Low sodium)

1 Head of cubed and chopped cauliflower

3 Cups of chopped potatoes

4 Cups of onion

2 large carrots

½ Cup of celery

2 Tbsp of Raw Coconut Amino.

1 Tbsp of Coconuts oil.

Directions:

Pour the coconuts oil in the Instant Pot

Add all of your ingredients into the Instant Pot you liner you are using.

Lock the lid of your Instant Pot; seal the vent of the steam.

Press the button "Manual" and "Adjust" the time to 9 minutes of cooking time. Once the pressure is reached, then the countdown starts.

Add 2Teaspoons of cashew butter

Use the blender to mash the soup and add a few cups of kale for nutritional values

Garnish your soup; then ladle in serving bowls

Serve and enjoy your soup!

Nutrition:

Calories – 134

Protein – 6 g.

Fat – 8 g.

Carbs – 12 g.

Carrot Soup with Fowl

Preparation Time: 8 minutes

Cooking Time: 20 minutes

Servings: 4

Ingredients:

½ fowl or chicken

2 quarts of chicken broth

¼ Cup of coarsely chopped onion

½ Cup of coarsely chopped carrots

½ Cup of coarsely chopped celery

1 Teaspoon of saffron threads

¾ Cup of corn kernels

½ Cup of finely chopped celery

1 tablespoon of fresh chopped parsley

1 Cup of cooked egg noodles

Directions:

Start by combining all together the stewing chicken or fowl with the chicken broth in your Instant Pot

Press sauté and add the onions, the carrots, the celery and the saffron

Now, close the lid and set at high pressure for around 20 minutes

Once the timer beeps, remove the chicken and shred it from the bone and cut it into small pieces

Strain your saffron broth with a fine sieve and then add the celery, the corn, the parsley, and the cooked noodles to your broth.

Return your soup to simmer for a few minutes

Serve and enjoy a delicious and nutritious soup

Nutrition:

Calories – 154.4

Protein – 10.9 g.

Fat – 0.8 g.

Carbs – 27.2 g.

Instant Pot Angel Hair Soup

Preparation Time: 5 minutes

Cooking Time: 15 minutes

Servings: 4

Ingredients:

4 Cups of low sodium chicken broth

3 Tbsp of tomato sauce

½ lb of angel hair pasta

7 leaves of fresh basil

2 tbsp of olive oil

¼ Cup of parmesan cheese to serve

2 Peeled and diced carrots

1 Peeled and cubed potato

¼ Cup of chickpeas

Directions:

Pour the oil, and add the broth, the chickpeas, the carrots, the tomato sauce and the basil in your Instant Pot

Press sauté and let the ingredients simmer for around 5 minutes.

Add 1 and ½ cup of chicken broth or and close the lid of the Instant Pot.

Set at high pressure for around 10 minutes.

Once the timer beeps, quick release the pressure and stir in the angel's hair pasta.

Boil the ingredients for 5 minutes

Add the basil and let cook for another minute.

Serve in bowl with a sprinkle of Parmesan cheese and tortilla strips.

Serve and enjoy!

Nutrition:

Calories – 216

Protein – 12.4 g.

Fat – 3.8 g.

Carbs – 35.1 g.

Coconut Lime Soup

Preparation Time: 6 minutes

Cooking Time: 10 minutes

Servings: 3-4

Ingredients:

½ Tbsp of coconut Oil

1 Finely chopped onion

1 Teaspoon of ground coriander powder

1 Medium sized Cauliflower that are broken into large floret

3 Cups of Vegetable Broth

½ Cup of Coconut Milk

2-3 Tbsp of Lime Juice

1 Pinch of Salt to taste

Directions:

Start by heating the Instant Pot and set the Manual button to sauté mode and sauté the onion for 6 minutes.

Add the coriander and keep stirring for a couple of minutes.

Add the rest of the ingredients; from the cauliflower, the vegetable broth and the coconut milk; then stir the ingredients to combine them.

Lock the lid and set the timer to 10 minutes.

Once the timer sets off; press the button keep warm and release the pressure

Blend the ingredients with a blender until it becomes soft

Add the lime juice and adjust the salt to taste

Serve and enjoy your soup!

Nutrition:

Calories – 262.8

Protein – 22 g.

Fat – 12.7 g.

Carbs – 16 g.

Garlic Soup with Almonds

Preparation Time: 5 minutes

Cooking Time: 15 minutes

Servings: 3

Ingredients:

3 and ¼ cups of freezing water

2 and ¼ cups of blanched almonds

5 Peeled and minced cloves of garlic

1 Baguette (remove the crusts removed and cut it into pieces)

½ Cup of coconuts oil

2 And ½ tbsp of sherry vinegar

2 Drops of almond extract

1 Pinch of Kosher salt

Directions:

Start by combining the 2 cups of water in the Instant Processor with the almonds, the garlic, and the bread in the food processor.

Set the manual to the button Sauté; sauté the ingredients soften for around 5 minutes.

Add the remaining quantity of water, the coconut oil, the vinegar, the extract, and the salt.

Cancel the setting of the Sauté feature and set the timer to 10 minutes

Once the timer is off, release the pressure and blend the ingredients with the a food processor or blender

Garnish your soup with the halves of almonds.

Serve and enjoy your soup!

Nutrition:

Calories – 120

Protein – 7.1 g.

Fat – 13.4 g.

Carbs – 37.1 g.

Beef Noodle Soup

Preparation Time: 8 minutes

Cooking Time: 35 minutes

Servings: 4

Ingredients:

½ lb of beef shoulder

1 Tbsp of kosher salt

¼ Cup of fresh ground black pepper

½ Teaspoon of all spice

¼ Teaspoon of ground ginger

1 Tbsp of coconut oil

1 Piece of 1 inch of fresh ginger

4 Cups of chicken broth

¼ Cups of fish sauce

1 Medium head of bok choy

1 Head of cabbage

1 or 2 packages of Shriataki noodles

2 scallions

¼ Cup of cilantro

1 Cup of bean sprouts

Directions:

Cut the beef into one and small cubes of 1 inch each.

Blend all together the salt, the pepper, the all spice powder and the ginger.

Spice the quantity of beef cubes into the mixture of the spices.

Put the instant potto the feature sauté, and once it becomes hot; then stir in the beef and sauté it until it becomes brown.

Add the broth of chicken

Add the fish sauce and the ginger

Now, lock the lid over the Instant Pot and Put the instant potto the Beef. Feature Stew and cook it for around 30 minutes. Meanwhile; cut the bok choy, the Napa cabbage and the scallions

When the cooking process is complete and the timer of the Instant Pot gets off, vent your steam and remove its lid. Then set the feature of the Instant Pot to the mode sauté

Add the Napa cabbage, the bok choy and the scallion; then simmer for around 5 minutes

Drain your noodles and rinse it; then add it to your instant Pot. Let the ingredients simmer for around 2 minutes

Serve and enjoy your soup with cilantro for garnish and sprouts

Nutrition:

Calories – 204.4

Protein – 11.7 g.

Fat – 7.5 g.

Carbs – 27.8 g.

Lamb Stew

Preparation Time: 10 minutes

Cooking Time: 35 minutes

Servings: 5-6

Ingredients:

2 lbs of diced lamb stew meat

1 Large acorn squash

4 Medium carrots

2 Small yellow onions

2 Rosemary Sprigs.

1 bay leaf

6 sliced or minced cloves of garlic

3 Tbsp of broth or water

¼ Tbsp of sp salt (Adjust it to taste)

Directions:

Start by peeling and seeding, then cubing your acorn squash. You can use a nice trick which is to microwave the squash for 2 minutes.

Slice the carrots into quite thick circles.

Peel your onions and cut it into halves; then slice it into the shape of half-moons.

Now, place all of your ingredients in the Instant Pot and set the feature Soup/ Stew button.

Lock the lid and set the timer to 35 minutes. When the timer goes off; release the steam and pressure before opening the lid.

Serve and enjoy your stew.

Nutrition:

Calories – 332.7

Protein – 28.9 g.

Fat – 6.9 g.

Carbs – 38.9 g.

Carrot Peanut Butter Soup

Preparation Time: 5 minutes

Cooking Time: 15 minutes

Servings: 4

Ingredients:

8 carrots, peeled and chopped

1 onion, chopped

3 garlic cloves, peeled

14 oz. coconut milk

1 ½ cup chicken stock

¼ cup peanut butter

1 tbsp. curry paste

Pepper

Salt

Directions:

Add all ingredients except salt and pepper into instant pot and stir well.

Secure pot with lid and cook on manual   high pressure for 15 minutes.

Quick release pressure then open the lid.

Puree the soup using an immersion blender until smooth.

Season soup with pepper and salt.

Serve and enjoy.

Nutrition:

Calories – 416

Protein – 8.2 g.

Fat – 34.2 g.

Carbs – 25.3 g.

Healthy Chicken Vegetable Soup

Preparation Time: 5 minutes

Cooking Time: 14 minutes

Servings: 6

Ingredients:

2 chicken breasts, cut into cubes

½ tsp. red pepper flakes

¼ cup fresh parsley, chopped

1 tsp. garlic powder

3 cups chicken broth

14 oz. can tomatoes, diced

¼ cup cabbage, shredded

1 cup frozen green beans

¼ cup frozen peas

½ cup frozen corn

2 celery stalks, chopped

1 carrot, peeled and cubed

½ sweet potato, peeled and cubed

3 garlic cloves, minced

½ onion, chopped

½ tsp. pepper

1 tsp. salt

Directions:

Add all ingredients into instant pot and stir well.
Secure pot with lid and cook on manual   high
pressure for 4 minutes.

Allow pressure to release naturally for 10 minutes,
then release using quick release Directions.

Stir well and serve.

Nutrition:

Calories – 171

Protein – 18.9 g.

Fat – 4.6 g.

Carbs – 13.9 g.

Chicken Rice Noodle Soup

Preparation Time: 5 minutes

Cooking Time: 10 minutes

Servings: 6

Ingredients:

6 cups chicken, cooked and cubed

3 tbsp. rice vinegar

2 ½ cups cabbage, shredded

2 tbsp. fresh ginger, grated

2 tbsp. soy sauce

3 garlic cloves, minced

8 oz. rice noodles

1 bell pepper, chopped

1 large carrot, peeled and sliced

6 cups chicken stock

2 celery stalks, sliced

1 onion, chopped

½ tsp. black pepper

Directions:

Add all ingredients into instant pot and stir well.

Secure pot with lid and cook on manual   high

pressure for 10 minutes.

Quick release pressure then open the lid.

Stir well and serve.

Nutrition:

Calories – 306

Protein – 43.1 g.

Fat – 5.1 g.

Carbs – 18.7 g.

Creamy Squash Soup

Preparation Time: 5 minutes

Cooking Time: 15 minutes

Servings: 4

Ingredients:

4 lbs. butternut squash, peeled, seeded, and cubed

4 cups beef stock

½ tsp. sage

1 tsp. thyme

2 garlic cloves, minced

1 onion, chopped

2 tbsp. olive oil

Pepper

Salt

Directions:

Add oil into instant pot and set on Sauté mode.

Add garlic and onion to the pot. Sauté for 5 minutes.

Add sage, thyme, pepper and salt. Stir for a minute.

Add squash and stock. Stir well.

Secure pot with lid and cook on manual   high pressure for 10 minutes.

Quick release pressure then open the lid.

Puree the soup using an immersion blender until smooth and creamy.

Serve and enjoy.

Nutrition:

Calories – 295

Protein – 7.7 g.

Fat – 8.1 g.

Carbs – 56.4 g.

Spicy Mushroom Soup

Preparation Time: 5 minutes

Cooking Time: 11 minutes

Servings: 2

Ingredients:

1 cup mushrooms, chopped

½ tsp. chili powder

2 tsp. garam masala

3 tbsp. olive oil

1 tsp. fresh lemon juice

5 cups chicken stock

¼ cup fresh celery, chopped

2 garlic cloves, crushed

1 onion, chopped

½ tsp. black pepper

1 tsp. sea salt

Directions:

Add oil into instant pot and set on Sauté mode.

Add garlic and onion to the pot. Sauté for 5 minutes.

Add chili powder and garam masala. Cook for a minute.

Add remaining ingredients and stir well.

Secure pot with lid and cook on manual   high pressure for 5 minutes.

Quick release pressure then open the lid.

Puree the soup using a blender and serve.

Nutrition:

Calories – 244

Protein – 3.9 g.

Fat – 22.8 g.

Carbs – 10.2 g.

Kale Beef Soup

Preparation Time: 15 minutes

Cooking Time: 43 minutes

Servings: 4

Ingredients:

1 lb. beef stew meat

1 tsp. cayenne pepper

3 garlic cloves, crushed

4 cups chicken broth

2 tbsp. olive oil

1 cup kale, chopped

1 onion, sliced

¼ tsp. black pepper

½ tsp. salt

Directions:

Add oil into instant pot and set on Sauté mode.

Add garlic and onion. Sauté for 3 minutes.

Add meat and sauté for 5 minutes.

Add broth and season with cayenne pepper, pepper and salt. Stir well.

Secure pot with lid and cook on manual high pressure for 25 minutes.

Quick release pressure then open the lid.

Add kale and stir well. Sit for 10 minutes.

Stir well and serve.

Nutrition:

Calories – 333

Protein – 40.3 g.

Fat – 15.6 g.

Carbs – 6.3 g.

Creamy Cauliflower Soup

Preparation Time: 10 minutes

Cooking Time: 32 minutes

Servings: 4

Ingredients:

2 cups cauliflower florets

1 tsp. pumpkin pie spice

5 cups chicken broth

3 tbsp. olive oil

1 onion, chopped

¼ tsp. salt

Directions:

Add oil into instant pot and set on Sauté mode.

Add onion to the pot and sauté for 5 minutes.

Add cauliflower and cook for a minute. Add broth and season with sea salt.

Secure pot with lid and cook on manual   high pressure for 24 minutes.

Quick release pressure then open the lid.

Puree the soup using an immersion blender until smooth.

Add pumpkin pie spice and stir well. Cook on Sauté mode for 2 minutes.

Serve and enjoy.

Nutrition:

Calories – 163

Protein – 7.4 g.

Fat – 12.3 g.

Carbs – 6.7 g.

Kale Cottage Cheese Soup

Preparation Time: 5 minutes

Cooking Time: 5 minutes

Servings: 4

Ingredients:

5 cups fresh kale, chopped

1 tbsp. olive oil

1 cup cottage cheese, cut into small chunks

3 cups chicken broth

½ tsp. black pepper

½ tsp. sea salt

Directions:

Add all ingredients except cottage cheese into instant pot and stir well.

Secure pot with lid and cook on manual   high pressure for 5 minutes.

Quick release pressure then open the lid.

Add cottage cheese and stir well.

Serve hot and enjoy.

Nutrition:

Calories – 152

Protein – 13.9 g.

Fat – 5.6 g. Carbs – 11.7 g.

Simple Kale Chicken Soup

Preparation Time: 5 minutes

Cooking Time: 15 minutes

Servings: 4

Ingredients:

2 cups chicken breast, cooked and chopped

2 tsp. garlic, minced

½ tsp. cinnamon

4 cups vegetable broth

1 onion, diced

12 oz. kale

1 tsp. salt

Directions:

Add all ingredients into instant pot and stir well.

Secure pot with lid and cook on manual   high
pressure for 5 minutes.

Allow pressure to release naturally for 10 minutes,
then release using quick release Directions.

Stir well and serve warm.

Nutrition:

Calories – 158

Protein – 19.7 g.

Fat – 2.8 g. Carbs – 13.1 g.

Mushroom Chicken Soup

Preparation Time: 10 minutes

Cooking Time: 25 minutes

Servings: 4

Ingredients:

1 lb. chicken breast, cut into chunks

1 tsp. Italian seasoning

2 ½ cups chicken stock

1 small yellow squash, chopped

2 cups mushrooms, sliced

2 garlic cloves, minced

1 onion, sliced

1 tsp. black pepper

1 tsp. salt

Directions:

Add all ingredients into instant pot and stir well.

Secure pot with lid and cook on manual   high

pressure for 15 minutes.

Allow pressure to release naturally for 10 minutes,

then release using quick release Directions.

Remove chicken from pot and puree the vegetable

mixture using a blender.

Shred the chicken using a fork. Return shredded chicken to the pot and stir well.

Serve and enjoy.

Nutrition:

Calories – 166

Protein – 26.4 g.

Fat – 3.8 g.

Carbs – 6.1 g.

Coconut Chicken Soup

Preparation Time: 5 minutes

Cooking Time: 15 minutes

Servings: 4

Ingredients:

1 lb. chicken thighs, boneless and cut into chunks

2 cups Swiss chard, chopped

1 ½ cups celery stalks, chopped

1 tsp. turmeric

1 tbsp. chicken broth base

10 oz. can tomato

1 cup coconut milk

1 tbsp. ginger, grated

4 garlic cloves, minced

1 onion, chopped

Directions:

Add ½ cup of coconut milk, broth base, turmeric, tomatoes, ginger, garlic and onion to the blender; blend until smooth.

Transfer blended the mixture to the instant pot along with Swiss chard, celery and chicken. Stir well.

Secure pot with lid and cook on manual   high pressure for 5 minutes.

Allow pressure to release naturally for 10 minutes, then release using quick release Directions.

Add remaining coconut oil and stir well.

Serve and enjoy.

Nutrition:

Calories – 473

Protein – 39.5 g.

Fat – 23.9 g.

Carbs – 29.7 g.

Taco Cheese Soup

Preparation Time: 10 minutes

Cooking Time: 25 minutes

Servings: 8

Ingredients:

1 lb. ground beef

1 lb. ground pork

½ cup Monterey Jack cheese, grated

2 tbsp. parsley, chopped

4 cups beef broth

20 oz. can tomatoes

16 oz. cream cheese

2 tbsp. taco seasonings

Directions:

Add both the ground meats in the instant pot and sauté for 10 minutes.

Add taco seasonings, tomatoes and cream cheese. Stir to combine.

Secure pot with lid and cook on manual   high pressure for 15 minutes.

Quick release pressure then open the lid.

Add parsley and stir well. Top with grated cheese and serve.

Nutrition:

Calories – 445

Protein – 41.1 g.

Fat – 28.1 g.

Carbs – 5.7 g.

Asparagus Garlic Ham Soup

Preparation Time: 15 minutes

Cooking Time: 50 minutes

Servings: 4

Ingredients:

1 ½ lbs. asparagus, chopped

4 cups chicken stock

2 tsp. garlic, minced

3 tbsp. olive oil

1 onion, diced

¾ cup ham, diced

½ tsp. thyme

Directions:

Add oil into instant pot and set on Sauté mode.

Add onion and sauté for 4 minutes.

Add garlic and ham and cook for a minute.

Add stock and thyme. Stir well.

Seal pot with lid and cook on Soup mode for 45 minutes.

Quick release pressure then open the lid,

Stir well and serve.

Nutrition:

Calories – 188

Protein – 9 g.

Fat – 13.5 g.

Carbs – 11.4 g.

Asian Pork Soup

Preparation Time: 10 minutes

Cooking Time: 30 minutes

Servings: 5

Ingredients:

1 lb. ground pork

1 tsp. ground ginger

¼ cup soy sauce

4 cups beef broth

½ cabbage head, chopped

2 carrots, peeled and shredded

1 onion, chopped

1 tbsp. olive oil

Pepper

Salt

Directions:

Add oil into instant pot and set on Sauté mode.

Add meat to the pot and sauté for 5 minutes.

Add remaining ingredients and stir well.

Secure pot with lid and cook on manual   high pressure for 25 minutes.

Quick release pressure then open the lid.

Stir well and serve hot.

Nutrition:

Calories – 229

Protein – 29.8 g.

Fat – 7.2 g.

Carbs – 10.6 g.

Creamy Potato Soup

Preparation Time: 5 minutes

Cooking Time: 9 minutes

Servings: 6

Ingredients:

3 lbs. russet potatoes, peeled and diced

15 oz. can coconut milk

3 cups chicken broth

½ tsp. dried thyme

2 carrots, peeled and sliced

3 garlic cloves, minced

1 onion, chopped

2 tbsp. olive oil

Pepper

Salt

Directions:

Add oil into instant pot and set on Sauté mode.

Add onion and garlic. Sauté for 3-4 minutes.

Add the rest of the ingredients except for coconut milk and stir well.

Secure pot with lid and cook on manual   high pressure for 9 minutes.

Quick release pressure then open the lid.

Puree the soup using an immersion blender until smooth.

Add coconut milk and stir well.

Season soup with pepper and salt.

Serve and enjoy.

Nutrition:

Calories – 373

Protein – 20.7 g.

Fat – 20.7 g.

Carbs – 42.3 g.

Chickpea Instant Pot Soup

Preparation Time: 10 minutes

Cooking Time: 25 minutes

Servings: 6

Ingredients:

2 cups of dry chickpeas

2 tablespoons extra virgin olive oil

1 yellow onion, chopped

3 garlic cloves, minced

salt to taste

2 carrots, chopped

1 green bell pepper, cored and chopped

3-4 red chili peppers

1 teaspoon ground coriander

1 teaspoon ground cumin

a teaspoon of Aleppo pepper (A Middle Eastern spice)

½ teaspoon of ground turmeric

½ teaspoon of ground allspice

15 ounces of chopped tomatoes with the juice

6 cups of low-sodium vegetable broth

juice from 1 lemon

1-ounce fresh cilantro, chopped

Directions:

Place the dry chickpeas in a bowl and submerge them in water. Let them soak overnight and then drain well.

Preheat your instant pot using the saute setting and adjust the heat to high. Put in the extra virgin olive oil and heat until simmering. Add the onions, garlic, and a pinch of salt. Cook for 3 minutes, while stirring regularly.

Add the carrots, bell peppers, and spices. Cook for another 4 minutes, while stirring until the vegetables have softened a bit.

Add the chickpeas, tomatoes, and the broth. Make sure to add the juice from the tomatoes too. Lock the instant pot lid, and put the pressure cooking setting on high. Set a timer for 15 minutes.

After cooking, allow natural release of pressure. After 10 minutes, you can press the quick release to remove any extra pressure.

Carefully unlock and remove the lid. Mix in the lemon juice and fresh cilantro.

Transfer the contents to serving bowls and drizzle a little extra olive oil.

Nutrition:

Calories – 367

Protein – 20.1 g.

Fat – 9.8 g.

Carbs – 12.1 g.

Instant Pot Mediterranean Chicken And Quinoa Stew

Preparation Time: 10 minutes

Cooking Time: 20 minutes

Servings: 6

Ingredients:

1-¼ pounds of chicken thighs, boneless and skinless

4 cups of butternut squash, peeled and chopped

4 cups unsalted chicken stock

1 cup yellow onion, chopped

2 garlic cloves, chopped

1 bay leaf

1-¼ teaspoons of kosher salt

1 teaspoon of dried oregano

1 teaspoon of ground fennel seeds

½ cup of uncooked quinoa

1-ounce of olives, sliced and pitted

Directions:

Combine the chicken, squash, stock, onion, garlic, bay leaf, salt, ground fennel seeds, oregano, and pepper in your instant pot. Cover the lid, turn the valve to seal and cook on high pressure for 8 minutes.

Release the valve carefully, using mitts or tongs. Quick-release until the steam and pressure go down. Remove chicken, then add quinoa to the instant pot, turn to saute and cook while occasionally stirring until the quinoa is tender. Shred the chicken and stir into stew. Discard bay leaf.

Serve the soup up into separate bowls, and sprinkle sliced olives.

Nutrition:

Calories – 243

Protein – 25 g.

Fat – 6 g.

Carbs – 24 g.

Greek Vegetable Soup

Preparation Time: 15 minutes

Cooking Time: 40 minutes

Servings: 4

Ingredients:

3 tablespoons of olive oil

1 onion, chopped

1 clove garlic, minced

3 cups of cabbage, shredded

2 medium carrots, chopped

2 celery stocks, chopped

2 cups of cooked chickpeas

4 cups of vegetable broth

15-ounce fire-roasted tomatoes, diced

salt and pepper to taste

Directions:

Put the olive oil in the instant pot and set to medium heat saute.

Add the onions and cook until soft. Add garlic and cabbage and cook for another 5 minutes. When the cabbage softens, add the carrots, celery, and chickpeas. Stir everything to combine and cook for 5 minutes longer

Add the broth and canned tomatoes, then season with salt and pepper.

Press cancel to end saute mode and cover the pot with the lid set to sealing mode.

Set to soup mode and adjust the time to 10 minutes.

After completion, release the pressure manually and serve immediately.

You may garnish the soup with parsley, feta, or anything you like on soup

Nutrition:

Calories – 412.9

Protein – 6.3 g.

Fat – 26.1 g.

Carbs – 43.2 g.

Instant Pot Mediterranean Lentil and Collard Soup

Preparation Time: 10 minutes

Cooking Time: 20 minutes

Servings: 6

Ingredients:

2 tablespoons of extra virgin olive oil

1 medium yellow onion, chopped

2 medium celery stocks, diced

3 garlic cloves, minced

2 teaspoons of ground cumin

1 teaspoon of ground turmeric

4 cups of low-sodium vegetable broth

1 ¼ cup of water

1 1/2 cups brown lentils, rinsed in water

2 carrots, peeled and diced

1 bay leaf

1 teaspoon himalayan salt

½ teaspoon of ground black pepper

3 collard leaves, cut into strips

1 teaspoon of lemon juice

Directions:

Set instant pot to saute, then add the olive oil, heat, and add onions and celery. Stir often for 5 minutes. Turn the instant pot off.

Stir in the garlic, cumin, and turmeric until combined.

Add broth, water, lentils, carrots, bay leaf, salt, and pepper. Lock the lid and close the valve. Fix to manual and cook on high pressure for 13 minutes. After completion, quick release the pressure, carefully remove the lid and stir in collards and lemon juice.

Make sure to lock the lid and set to manual and cook for 2 more minutes on high. Quick-release the pressure, open the lid, and it's ready to serve.

Nutrition:

Calories – 127.9

Protein – 7.3 g.

Fat – 0.8 g.

Carbs – 25.9 g.

Green Chicken Chili

Preparation Time: 10 minutes

Cooking Time: 35 minutes

Servings: 8

Ingredients:

2 tbsp. unsalted butter

1 medium yellow onion (to be peeled and chopped)

½ lb. poblano peppers (to be seeded and roughly chopped)

½ lb. Anaheim peppers (to be seeded and roughly chopped)

½ lb. tomatillos (to be husked and quartered)

2 small jalapeño peppers (to be seeded and roughly chopped)

2 garlic cloves (to be peeled and minced)

1 tsp. ground cumin

6 bone-in, skin-on chicken thighs (2 ½ lbs.
in total)

2 cups chicken stock

2 cups water

1/3 cup roughly chopped fresh cilantro

3 cans Great Northern beans (to be drained and
rinsed, 15 oz. cans)

Directions:

Choose the "Sauté" button on the Instant Pot and
when hot, add butter to melt. Once the butter
melts, add onion and cook for about 3 minutes
until softened. Add poblano and Anaheim peppers,
then tomatillos, and jalapeños. Cook 3 minutes
add garlic and cumin. Cook about 30 seconds or
until fragrant. Then cancel sautéing.

Add the thighs, stock, and water to pot and stir. Tightly close lid and have the steam release set to the "Sealing" position. Select the "Rice/Grain" option and set the timer for 30 minutes. At the end of the cook time, do a quick release of pressure and open lid to stir well. Press the "Cancel" button and transfer the chicken to a cutting board. After carefully removing the skin, shred the meat with two forks.

Using an immersion blender, purée the sauce until smooth. Stir in the meat, cilantro, and beans and serve warm.

Nutrition:

Calories – 304

Protein – 33 g.

Fat – 10 g.

Carbs – 19 g.

Instant Pot Italian Beef Stew

Preparation Time: 10 minutes

Cooking Time: 35 minutes

Servings: 6

Ingredients:

3 pounds of beef stew

1 onion, diced

4 carrots, diced

8-ounce baby portabella mushrooms, sliced

24-ounces of beef broth

15 ounce diced tomatoes, canned

3 tablespoons of white flour

1 teaspoon of dried basil leaves

1 teaspoon of dried thyme leaves

1 teaspoon of salt

1 teaspoon of pepper

dried parsley

Directions:

Place meat in the instant pot.

Add in carrots, broth, flour, basil, thyme, salt, pepper, and tomatoes to instant pot and stir.

Close the lid.

Cook on high pressure for 35 minutes.

Quick release the pressure and carefully remove the lid.

Stir in the mushroom, stir the soup and then serve.

Nutrition:

Calories – 385

Protein – 54 g.

Fat – 12 g.

Carbs – 12 g.

Instant Pot Fish Stew

Preparation Time: 5 minutes

Cooking Time: 15 minutes

Servings: 4

Ingredients:

4 tablespoons of extra-virgin olive oil

1 medium red onion, chopped

4 garlic cloves, chopped

½ cup of dry white wine

8-ounce clam juice

2 1/2 cups of water

½ pound potatoes, diced

1 1/2 cups of fresh tomatoes with juices

kosher salt

black pepper for taste

pinch of crushed red pepper for taste

2 pounds sea bass cut into 2-inch pieces

2 tablespoons lemon juice

2 tablespoons of fresh dill, chopped

Directions:

Use saute setting on your instant pot and cook onions in 2 tablespoons of olive oil for 3 minutes, until golden brown.

Add the chopped garlic, saute until fragrant.
Add the white wine, scrape up any brown bits,
until about half of the wine has evaporated.
Add the clam juice, water, potatoes, tomatoes,
salt, pepper, and a pinch of crushed red pepper.
Turn the saute off, cover and seal your instant
pot, and set to manual high pressure for 5
minutes.

After this, quick release the pressure. Open the
instant pot and turn the saute setting back on.
Once the soup is simmering, add the pieces of
fish, and simmer for about 5 minutes, until the
fish flakes apart easily.

Turn off saute mode, stir in lemon juice and fresh
dill and remaining olive oil. Season to taste and
serve.

Nutrition:

Calories – 471

Protein – 43 g.

Fat – 20 g.

Carbs – 24 g.

Crushed Lentil Soup

Preparation Time: 10 minutes

Cooking Time: 30 minutes

Servings: 8

Ingredients:

2 tablespoons vegetable broth

1 onion, finely chopped

4 garlic cloves, minced

4 cups unsalted vegetable broth

2 cups of water

2 cups red split lentils

1 small pinch saffron

1 teaspoon coriander

1 teaspoon cumin

½ teaspoon freshly ground black pepper

1 teaspoon sea salt

½ teaspoon of red pepper flakes

2 bay leaves

2 tablespoons fresh lemon juice

Directions:

Put the instant potto saute, add the vegetable broth, 2 tablespoons. Then put in the garlic and onions and cook until they are soft, about 4-5 minutes.

Add remaining ingredients except for bay leaves and lemon juice. Stir and then lock the lid of the instant pot.

Press cancel and choose the soup function. Set timer for 30 minutes. After the 30 minutes, let it sit for another 20 minutes to release the pressure. Open the lid and add bay leaves and lemon juice, then stir for 5 minutes.

Remove bay leaves and serve.

Nutrition:

Calories – 191

Protein – 11.8 g.

Fat – 1.2 g.

Carbs – 34.4 g.

Lemony Lentil Soup

Preparation Time: 10 minutes

Cooking Time: 25 minutes

Servings: 4

Ingredients:

1 tablespoon of olive oil

1 medium onion, peeled and diced

2 carrots, diced

5 garlic cloves, minced

6 cups of vegetable stock

1 1/2 cup of red lentils

⅔ cup of whole kernel corn

2 teaspoons of ground cumin

1 teaspoon of curry powder

zest and juice of 1 lemon

sea salt and black pepper to taste

Directions:

Choose the saute function on your instant pot and add oil. Add the onions and carrots and saute for 5 minutes. Stir occasionally until the onions are soft and translucent. Add garlic and saute for 1 more minute, until fragrant.

Pour in the vegetable stock, lentils, corn, cumin, and curry powder until combined

Make sure to lock the lid and set to "sealing." Press and set for manual high pressure, and adjust the timer for 8 minutes. Cook, then carefully turn to venting for quick release. Once vented, remove the lid carefully.

Using a blender, puree the soup until it reaches your desired consistency.

Return the puree to the instant pot and stir in lemon zest and juice until combined.

Season with sea salt and black pepper to taste. Serve warm.

Nutrition:

Calories – 260

Protein – 16 g.

Fat – 6 g.

Carbs – 40 g.

Instant Pot Vegetable Soup

Preparation Time: 10 minutes

Cooking Time: 20 minutes

Servings: 5

Ingredients:

2 tablespoons extra virgin olive oil

½ onion, chopped

½ green bell pepper, chopped

2 cloves garlic, minced

1 1/2 cups green cabbage, chopped

1 1/2 cups small cauliflower florets

1 cup chopped carrots

½ cup green beans, cut into small pieces

4 cups low-sodium vegetable broth

1 can diced tomatoes, no salt added

1 bay leaf

½ teaspoon salt

4 cups of chopped spinach

15 ounce cannellini beans, rinsed

¼ cup chopped basil

Directions:

Place olive oil in the instant pot and set to saute. Add onions, bell peppers, and garlic, then cook, stirring often until starting to soften, which will take 2-3 minutes.

Put in the carrots, cauliflower, cabbage, and green beans and cook for 4-5 minutes, stirring often.

Add the broth, tomatoes, bay leaf, and salt. Turn off the heat, lock the lid, and cook on high for 5 minutes.

Release the pressure using quick release, open the lid carefully, and remove bay leaf. Stir in the spinach, basil, and beans.

Ready to serve. May drizzle more olive oil on top if desired.

Nutrition:

Calories – 192

Protein – 7.3 g.

Fat – 6.6 g.

Carbs – 26 g.

Instant Pot Golden Lentil and Spinach Soup

Preparation Time: 10 minutes

Cooking Time: 25 minutes

Servings: 4

Ingredients:

2 teaspoons of olive oil

½ yellow onion, diced

2 carrots, peeled and diced

1 celery stock, diced

4 garlic cloves, minced

2 teaspoons ground cumin

1 teaspoon ground turmeric

1 teaspoon dried thyme

1 teaspoon kosher salt

¼ teaspoon freshly ground black pepper

1 cup dry brown lentils, rinsed well

4 cups low-sodium vegetable broth

8 ounces baby spinach

Directions:

Choose saute function of the instant pot and add oil. When hot, add onions, carrots, and celery. Saute, occasionally stirring, until tender, about 5 minutes.

Add garlic, cumin, turmeric, thyme, salt, and pepper. Cook and stir for one minute.

Stir in lentil and broth.

Place lid on instant pot and put the valve to "sealing." Press manual high pressure and set a timer for 12 minutes.

After 12 minutes, quick release pressure and then carefully remove the lid when done. Stir in the spinach, and add salt and pepper to taste.

Nutrition:

Calories – 134

Protein – 9 g.

Fat – 3 g.

Carbs – 17 g.

Mediterranean Bamyeh Okra Tomato Stew

Preparation Time: 5 minutes

Cooking Time: 7 minutes

Servings: 4

Ingredients:

¼ cup of water

2 tablespoons apple cider vinegar

1 cup onions, chopped

1 tablespoon minced garlic

14.5 ounce canned tomatoes

1 tablespoon vegetable broth

1 teaspoon smoked paprika

½ teaspoon ground allspice

1 teaspoon salt

1 1/2 pounds fresh okra

Directions:

Place all ingredients except for the lemon juice and tomato paste into instant pot. Put in okra last. Cook on high pressure for 2 minutes, let it rest for 5 minutes.

Quick release the pressure.

Open the lid carefully and add tomato paste in water and then the lemon juice. Stir gently and serve.

Nutrition:

Calories – 85

Protein – 4 g.

Fat – 5 g.

Carbs – 19 g.

Instant Pot Minestrone Soup

Preparation Time: 10 minutes

Cooking Time: 35 minutes

Servings: 6

Ingredients:

2 tablespoons olive oil

3 cloves garlic, minced

1 onion, diced

2 carrots, peeled and diced

2 celery stalks, diced

1 ½ teaspoons fresh basil

1 teaspoon dried oregano

½ teaspoon fennel seed

6 cups low-sodium chicken broth

28 ounce can tomatoes, diced

1 can kidney beans, drained and rinsed

1 zucchini, chopped

1 Parmesan rind

1 bay leaf

1 bunch kale, chopped and stems removed

2 teaspoons red wine vinegar

kosher salt and freshly ground black pepper

⅓ cup Parmesan, grated

2 tablespoons fresh parsley leaves, chopped

Directions:

Set instant pot to saute, add olive oil, garlic, onion, carrots, and celery. Cook, occasionally stirring, until tender. Stir in basil, oregano, and fennel seeds, for a minute, until fragrant.

Pour in the chicken stock, tomatoes, kidney beans, zucchini, parmesan rind, and bay leaf. Select the manual high pressure setting and set for 5 minutes.

When completed, press quick release to remove all pressure.

Stir in the kale for about 2 minutes, then stir in red wine vinegar and season with salt and pepper to taste. Ready to serve.

Nutrition:

Calories – 227

Protein – 14 g.

Fat – 7 g.

Carbs – 26 g.

Instant Pot Greek Beef Stew

Preparation Time: 15 minutes

Cooking Time: 40 minutes

Servings: 4

Ingredients:

1 ½ pounds stew beef cut into small cubes

¼ cup of butter

8 small onions

8 small potatoes

2-3 carrots, sliced

¾ cups tomato paste

1 teaspoon cinnamon

Directions:

Set instant pot to saute mode and cook beef in the butter until browned. This will take about 5 minutes. Then remove.

Put in the onions to the pot and saute about 5 minutes.

Stop saute mode. Add beef back to the pot and then add carrots, potatoes, tomato paste, and cinnamon. Add 2-3 cups of water.

Lock the lid and set pressure to high and cook for 35 minutes.

Allow steam to release naturally for 10 minutes and then quick release remaining pressure.

Ready to serve.

Nutrition:

Calories – 479

Protein – 43 g.

Fat – 20 g.

Carbs – 31 g.

Instant Pot Bean Soup

Preparation Time: 20 minutes

Cooking Time: 1 hour and 25 minutes

Servings: 6

Ingredients:

1 pound white beans

1 ¼ pound of beef shanks with bone

1 white onion, chopped

1 green bell pepper, chopped

2 carrots, chopped

4 tablespoons olive oil

2 tablespoons fresh parsley, chopped

½ teaspoon garlic, minced

½ tablespoon salt

1 can tomatoes, diced

1 liter water

3 bay leaves

½ teaspoon paprika

Directions:

Immerse beans in a bowl of cold water overnight.
Place the beef shanks and olive oil in instant pot
and turn on saute setting. Brown on both sides

Remove the beans from water, and rinse. Add beans, diced tomatoes, paprika, bay leaves, and garlic.

Add water, close the lid, and cook on the manual high setting for 1 hour. Make sure the beans are soft, and if not, cook for another 30 minutes. Serve.

Nutrition:

Calories – 86

Protein – 2.8 g.

Fat – 5 g.

Carbs – 9.7 g.

Chestnut Soup

Preparation Time: 10 minutes

Cooking Time: 25 minutes

Servings: 4

Ingredients:

½ pound fresh chestnuts

4 tablespoons butter

1 sprig sage

¼ teaspoon white pepper

¼ teaspoon nutmeg

1 onion, chopped

1 stalk celery, chopped

1 potato, chopped

2 tablespoons rum

2 tablespoons fresh cream

Directions:

Puree the fresh chestnuts in a blender.

Put the butter, onions, sage, celery and white pepper in the Instant Pot and select "Sauté".

Sauté for 4 minutes and add potato, stock and chestnuts.

Set the Instant Pot to "Soup" and cook for 15 minutes at high pressure.

Release the pressure naturally and add rum, nutmeg and fresh cream.

Blend the contents of the Instant Pot to a smooth consistency.

Nutrition:

Calories: 290;

Total Fat: 13.3g;

Carbs: 36.5g;

Sugars: 2.5g;

Protein: 3g

Tortilla and White Beans Soup

Preparation Time: 10 minutes

Cooking Time: 27 minutes

Servings: 4

Ingredients:

1 cup white beans

4 tablespoons butter

¼ teaspoon white pepper

1 onion, roughly sliced

1 tablespoon sun dried tomatoes

¼ cup fresh cream

4 cups water

2 teaspoons salt

1 carrot, roughly chopped

4 garlic cloves, minced

4 tablespoons tomato paste

Crunchy tortilla chips, for garnish

Directions:

Put the butter, garlic, carrots, onions and white pepper in the Instant Pot and select "Sauté". Sauté for 5 minutes and add white beans, potatoes, sun dried tomatoes, tomato paste, salt and water.

Set the Instant Pot to "Soup" and cook for 12 minutes at high pressure.

Release the pressure naturally and add sour cream.

Blend the contents of the Instant Pot to a smooth consistency and top with crunchy tortilla chips.

Nutrition:

Calories: 353;

Total Fat: 14.7g;

Carbs: 44.2g;

Sugars: 5.3g;

Protein: 14g

Vegetable Noodle Soup

Preparation Time: 8 minutes

Cooking Time: 20 minutes

Servings: 5

Ingredients:

½ cup potatoes, diced

½ cup peas

½ cup carrots

½ cup cauliflower

6 oz. noodles, cooked and drained

½ cup onions

3 garlic cloves, minced

½ inch ginger, minced

1 cup tomatoes, diced

10 oz. baby carrots

2 teaspoons Worcestershire sauce

32 oz. vegetable stock

1 tablespoon olive oil

1 teaspoon salt

1 teaspoon black pepper

Directions:

Put the oil, ginger, garlic, carrots, onions and cauliflowers in the Instant Pot and select "Sauté".

Sauté for 5 minutes and add potatoes, tomatoes, peas, vegetable stock and Worcestershire sauce.

Set the Instant Pot to "Soup" and cook for 12 minutes at high pressure.

Release the pressure naturally and add cooked noodles.

Season with salt and black pepper and serve immediately.

Nutrition:

Calories: 148;

Total Fat: 4g;

Carbs: 24.8g;

Sugars: 7.8g;

Protein: 4.6g

Manchow Soup

Preparation Time: 10 minutes

Cooking Time: 25 minutes

Servings: 4

Ingredients:

3 oz. fried noodles, for garnish

½ cup green bell peppers

½ cup bean sprouts

½ cup mushrooms

½ cup broccoli

½ cup baby carrots

2 green onions, chopped

4 garlic cloves, minced

½ inch ginger, minced

1 teaspoon soy sauce

1 teaspoon vinegar

2 teaspoons chilli sauce

3 cups vegetable stock

1 tablespoon oil

Salt and pepper, to taste

Roasted crushed peanuts, for garnish

Directions:

Put the oil, ginger, garlic, carrots, onions and carrots in the Instant Pot and select "Sauté". Sauté for 4 minutes and add soy sauce, chilli sauce, vinegar and vegetable stock.

Set the Instant Pot to "Soup" and cook for 10 minutes at high pressure.

Release the pressure naturally and add cooked noodles.

Season with salt and black pepper and garnish with fried noodles and crushed roasted peanuts.

Nutrition:

Calories: 379;

Total Fat: 20.8g;

Carbs: 43.6g;

Sugars: 2.4g;

Protein: 8.7g

Chinese Noodle Soup

Preparation Time: 10 minutes

Cooking Time: 30 minutes

Servings: 8

Ingredients:

12 oz. noodles, cooked and drained

1 cup red bell peppers

1 cup mushrooms

1 cup broccoli

1 cup bok choy

4 green onion whites

8 garlic cloves, minced

1 inch ginger, minced

2 teaspoons soy sauce

1 teaspoon white chilli vinegar

20 oz. baby carrots

2 teaspoons chilli sauce

8 cups vegetable stock

2 tablespoons oil

Salt and pepper, to taste

Onion greens, for garnish

Directions:

Put the oil, ginger, garlic, baby carrots and onions in the Instant Pot and select "Sauté".

Sauté for 4 minutes and add broccoli, bok choy, red bell peppers, mushrooms, soy sauce, chilli vinegar, chilli sauce and vegetable stock.

Set the Instant Pot to "Soup" and cook for 15 minutes at high pressure.

Release the pressure naturally and add cooked noodles.

Season with salt and black pepper and garnish with onion greens.

Nutrition:

Calories: 145;

Total Fat: 4.7g;

Carbs: 22.6g;

Sugars: 6.1g;

Protein: 4g

Japanese Udon Noodle Soup

Preparation Time: 10 minutes

Cooking Time: 27 minutes

Servings: 2

Ingredients:

3 oz. Japanese udon noodles, cooked and drained

½ cup green bell peppers

½ cup celery

½ cup mushrooms

½ cup bamboo shoots

2 garlic cloves, minced

½ green chilli, finely chopped

½ cup baby carrots

1 teaspoon rice vinegar soy sauce

½ inch ginger, minced

1 green onion white

1 teaspoon rice wine vinegar

1 teaspoon red chilli sauce

1 tablespoon sesame oil

Bean sprouts and green onions, for garnish

Salt and pepper, to taste

Directions:

Put the oil, ginger, garlic, baby carrots and onions in the Instant Pot and select "Sauté".

Sauté for 4 minutes and add bamboo shoots, celery, green bell peppers, mushrooms, soy sauce, rice wine vinegar, chilli sauce.

Set the Instant Pot to "Soup" and cook for 13 minutes at high pressure.

Release the pressure naturally and add cooked udon noodles.

Season with salt and black pepper and garnish with onion greens and bean sprouts.

Nutrition:

Calories: 179;

Total Fat: 3.9g;

Carbs: 30g;

Sugars: 2.7g;

Protein: 3.6g

Chestnut Bacon Soup

Preparation Time: 10 minutes

Cooking Time: 35 minutes

Servings: 4

Ingredients:

5 meatless bacon strips, cooked crispy

1 bay laurel leaf

½ pound fresh chestnuts

3 tablespoons butter

1 sprig sage

¼ teaspoon white pepper

¼ teaspoon nutmeg

1 onion, chopped

1 potato, chopped

2 tablespoons fresh cream

Directions:

Puree the fresh chestnuts in a blender.

Put the butter, onions, sage, celery and white pepper in the Instant Pot and select "Sauté".

Sauté for 4 minutes and add potato, bay laurel leaf, stock and chestnuts.

Set the Instant Pot to "Soup" and cook for 20 minutes at high pressure.

Release the pressure naturally and add nutmeg and fresh cream.

Blend the contents of the Instant Pot to a smooth consistency and serve with bacon.

Nutrition:

Calories: 435;

Total Fat: 25.4g;

Carbs: 37.7g;

Sugars: 2.4g;

Protein: 16.7g

Pearl Barley Soup

Preparation Time: 10 minutes

Cooking Time: 25 minutes

Servings: 66

Ingredients:

1 cup all-purpose flour

2 onions, chopped

2 celery stalks, chopped

2 carrots, chopped

4 tablespoons olive oil

2 cups mushroom, sliced

28 oz. vegetable stock

¾ cup pearl barley

2 teaspoons dried oregano

1 cup purple wine

Salt and pepper, to taste

Directions:

Put the oil, garlic and onions in the Instant Pot and select "Sauté".

Sauté for 3 minutes and add rest of the ingredients.

Set the Instant Pot to "Soup" and cook for 15 minutes at high pressure.

Release the pressure naturally and serve hot.

Nutrition:

Calories: 310;

Total Fat: 10.1g;

Carbs: 43.8g;

Sugars: 4.2g;

Protein: 6.6g

Conclusion

When you are on a diet trying to lose weight or manage a condition, you will be strictly confined to follow an eating plan. Such plans often place numerous demands on individuals: food may need to be boiled, other foods are forbidden, permitting you only to eat small portions and so on.

On the other hand, a lifestyle such as the Mediterranean diet is entirely stress-free. It is easy to follow because there are almost no restrictions. There is no time limit on the Mediterranean diet because it is more of a lifestyle than a diet. You do not need to stop at some point but carry on for the rest of your life. The foods that you eat under the Mediterranean model include unrefined cereals, white meats, and the occasional dairy products.

The Mediterranean lifestyle, unlike other diets, also requires you to engage with family and friends and share meals together. It has been noted that communities around the Mediterranean spend between one and two hours enjoying their meals. This kind of bonding between family members or friends helps bring people closer together, which helps foster closer bonds hence fewer cases of depression, loneliness, or stress, all of which are precursors to chronic diseases.

You will achieve many benefits using the Instant Pot Pressure Cooker. These are just a few instances you will discover in your Mediterranean-style recipes:

Pressure cooking means that you can (on average) cook meals 75% faster than boiling/braising on the stovetop or baking and roasting in a conventional oven.

This is especially helpful for vegan meals that entail the use of dried beans, legumes, and pulses. Instead of pre-soaking these ingredients for hours before use, you can pour them directly into the Instant Pot, add water, and pressure cook these for several minutes. However, always follow your recipe carefully since they have been tested for accuracy.

Nutrients are preserved. You can use your pressure-cooking techniques using the Instant Pot to ensure the heat is evenly and quickly distributed.

It is not essential to immerse the food into the water. You will provide plenty of water in the cooker for efficient steaming. You will also be saving the essential vitamins and minerals. The food won't become oxidized by the exposure of air or heat. Enjoy those fresh green veggies with their natural and vibrant colors.

The cooking elements help keep the foods fully sealed, so the steam and aromas don't linger throughout your entire home. That is a plus, especially for items such as cabbage, which throws out a distinctive smell.

You will find that beans and whole grains will have a softer texture and will have an improved taste. The meal will be cooked consistently since the Instant Pot provides even heat distribution.

You'll also save tons of time and money. You will be using much less water, and the pot is fully insulated, making it more energy-efficient when compared to boiling or steaming your foods on the stovetop. It is also less expensive than using a microwave, not to mention how much more flavorful the food will be when prepared in the Instant Pot cooker.

You can delay the cooking of your food items so you can plan ahead of time. You won't need to stand around as you await your meal. You can reduce the cooking time by reducing the 'hands-on' time. Just leave for work or a day of activities, and you will come home to a special treat.

In a nutshell, the Instant Pot is:

Easy To Use Healthy recipes for the entire family are provided.

You can make authentic one-pot recipes in your Instant Pot.

If you forget to switch on your slow cooker, you can make any meal done in a few minutes in your Instant Pot.

You can securely and smoothly cook meat from frozen.

It's a laid-back way to cook. You don't have to watch a pan on the stove or a pot in the oven.

The pressure cooking procedure develops delicious flavors swiftly.